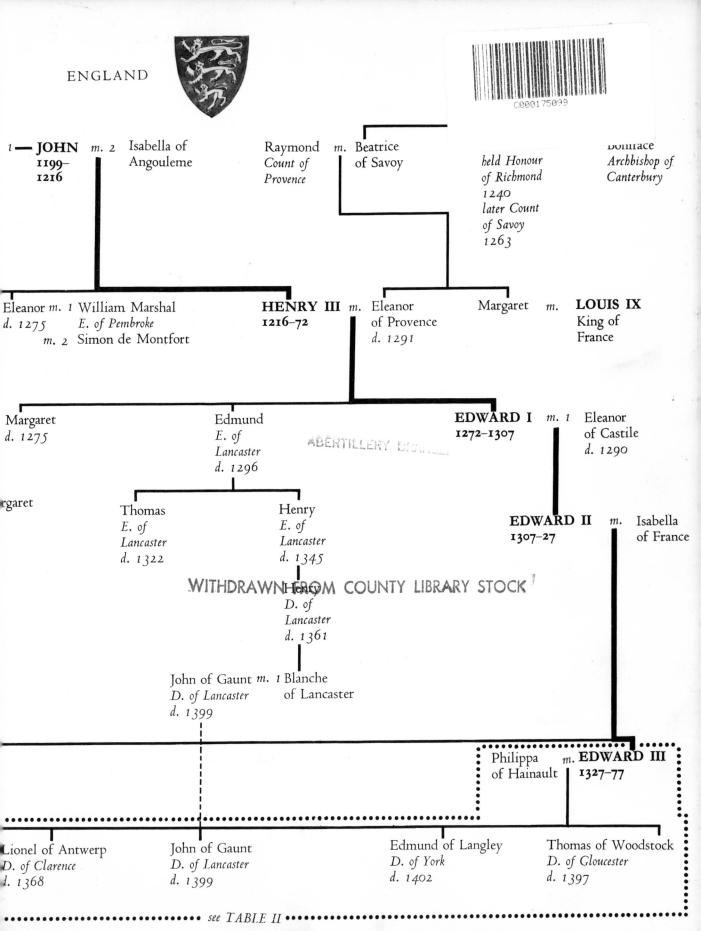

ENGLAND

C000175099

ABERTILLERY DISTRICT

WITHDRAWN FROM COUNTY LIBRARY STOCK

1 — **JOHN** 1199–1216 m. 2 Isabella of Angouleme

Raymond Count of Provence m. Beatrice of Savoy

held Honour of Richmond 1240 later Count of Savoy 1263

Boniface Archbishop of Canterbury

Eleanor d. 1275 m. 1 William Marshal E. of Pembroke m. 2 Simon de Montfort

HENRY III 1216–72 m. Eleanor of Provence d. 1291

Margaret m. **LOUIS IX** King of France

Margaret d. 1275

Edmund E. of Lancaster d. 1296

EDWARD I 1272–1307 m. 1 Eleanor of Castile d. 1290

Thomas E. of Lancaster d. 1322

Henry E. of Lancaster d. 1345

EDWARD II 1307–27 m. Isabella of France

Henry D. of Lancaster d. 1361

John of Gaunt D. of Lancaster d. 1399 m. 1 Blanche of Lancaster

Philippa of Hainault m. **EDWARD III** 1327–77

Lionel of Antwerp D. of Clarence d. 1368

John of Gaunt D. of Lancaster d. 1399

Edmund of Langley D. of York d. 1402

Thomas of Woodstock D. of Gloucester d. 1397

see TABLE II

ty Library

rteen

se,
ver,
our
n

559

WITHDRAWN FROM COUNTY LIBRARY STOCK

MEDIEVAL
BRITAIN

2

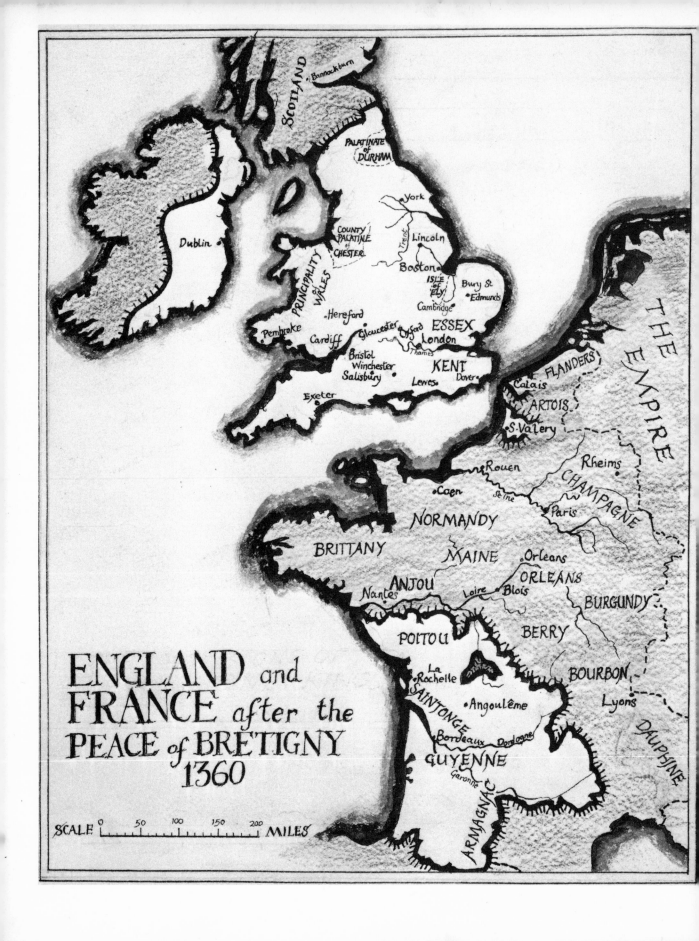

ENGLAND and FRANCE after the PEACE of BRETIGNY 1360

SCALE 0 50 100 150 200 MILES

MEDIEVAL
BRITAIN

TEXT BY HENRY LOYN

DRAWINGS BY ALAN SORRELL AND
RICHARD SORRELL

LUTTERWORTH PRESS · GUILDFORD AND LONDON

First published 1977

In the same series

PREHISTORIC BRITAIN
Text by Barbara Green, Drawings by Alan Sorrell

ROMAN BRITAIN
Text by Aileen Fox, Drawings by Alan Sorrell

SAXON ENGLAND
Text by John Hamilton, Drawings by Alan Sorrell

NORMAN BRITAIN
Text by Henry Loyn, Drawings by Alan Sorrell

All Rights Reserved.   No part of this publication
may be reproduced, stored in a retrieval system,
or transmitted, in any form or by any means,
electronic, mechanical, photocopying, recording
or otherwise, without the prior permission of
Lutterworth Press, Farnham Road, Guildford, Surrey.

Text set in 14 on 17 Monotype Centaur Roman:
captions set in 12 on 12 Monotype Centaur Italic

A19659
5942.03

ISBN 0 7188 2153 X

Text copyright © 1977 by Henry Loyn
Drawings copyright © 1977 by Richard Sorrell and the estate of Alan Sorrell

PRINTED IN GREAT BRITAIN
BY FLETCHER & SON LTD,
NORWICH

CONTENTS

The coin on the half-title is a groat of the reign of Edward I (1272–1307).

The drawing on the title page shows the Coronation Chair from Westminster Abbey, which dates from the time of Edward I. Set into the Chair is the Stone of Scone on which the Scottish kings were crowned; the Stone was seized by Edward I during the Scottish wars and brought south to London, where it has since remained.

The genealogical table on the front endpapers shows the royal houses of Scotland and England from the late twelfth to the late fourteenth century.

The genealogical table on the back endpapers shows the houses of Lancaster and York in the fifteenth century.

The drawing on page 48 shows the "Bishop's Eye" window, Lincoln.

To

ALAN SORRELL

1904—1974

SOME OTHER BOOKS

ABOUT MEDIEVAL BRITAIN

There are many good guides to the Later Middle Ages including three volumes in the *Oxford History of England* (May McKisack's *Fourteenth Century*, Oxford, 1959, is especially valuable). A mass of original material in translation is now available in two volumes of the *English Historical Documents* series published by Eyre Methuen (vol. III, 1189–1327, ed. H. Rothwell (1975) and vol. IV, 1327–1485, ed. A. R. Myers (1969)). Reliable general accounts are to be found in George Holmes, *The Later Middle Ages, 1272–1485*, Nelson, 1962, and B. Wilkinson, *The Later Middle Ages in England*, Longmans, 1969. On the fifteenth century, S. B. Chrimes, *Lancastrians, Yorkists and Henry VII*, Macmillan, 1964, and C. D. Ross, *The Wars of the Roses*, Thames and Hudson, 1976, are valuable. C. D. Ross also provides a full and up-to-date biography of *Edward IV*, Eyre Methuen, 1974. Social history is ably discussed by A. R. Myers, *England in the Later Middle Ages*, Pelican, 1952. A rich introduction to visual material is given in the *Oxford History of English Art* by J. Brieger, 1216–1307, Oxford, 1957, and by Joan Evans, 1307–1441, Oxford, 1949.

The following pamphlets published by the Historical Association (59A, Kennington Park Road, London) will also be found useful: C. H. Knowles, *Simon de Montfort*, E. Miller, *The Origins of Parliament*, C. T. Allmand, *Henry V*.

1. *Pembroke Castle: the cylindrical keep was built by William Marshall, c. 1200 A.D.*

KING AND BARONS: FROM MAGNA CARTA TO THE DEATH OF HENRY III

THE early thirteenth century was a time when England suffered a period of great political unrest. Under King John (1199–1216) it was a much-governed land, but the character of the king, the loss of Normandy in 1204, and bitter quarrels with the Papacy led to baronial revolt and the consequent granting of Magna Carta (the great Charter) in June 1215. Magna Carta is best remembered as an assertion of the principle that the king should rule according to law, rather than as a precise statement of English liberties. Uncertainty remained on the question of what part the barons should play in royal government, and what steps should be taken to prevent abuse of royal powers.

The Civil War which followed the granting of Magna Carta did not end with the death of King John on October 18, 1216. His nine-year-old son, Henry, succeeded to a perilous heritage. Prince Louis (later Louis VIII), the son and heir of the French king, controlled half of England, and the English baronage was divided in sympathies. Thanks to the loyalty of some of the great barons, notably William Marshal, Ranulf of Chester and Hubert de Burgh, the young king survived, and his advisers were able to make a firm peace with France. The Papacy also gave support through strong legates, and barons and clergy

alike showed skill in the novel task of establishing stable royal rule during a king's minority. They did not question the ultimate power of the king, and throughout his long reign—though at times stubborn and wayward—Henry III (1216–72) proved a staunch and surprisingly successful defender of royal rights.

The king's government was therefore carried out efficiently and with only minor disturbance during his minority and during an early period of personal rule. In 1236 Henry married a French princess, Eleanor of Provence, whose sister had married the French king, Louis IX. The politics of the succeeding generation often revolved around the

2. (Facing page) In a sea battle in August 1217, a strong French fleet, which suffered heavy loss, was beaten back from the Thames estuary to Calais.

3. (Below) Tournaments became more popular among the baronial class and more formal in the thirteenth century.

4. (Above) When Parliaments were held at Westminster, the Commons often met at the Chapter House of Westminster Abbey. De Montfort held his great Parliament in London, January—March 1265.

5. (Facing page) Roger Bacon was learned in theology and philosophy as well as in science. Because of suspected heresies in his teaching, he spent much of his later years in prison.

question of foreign favourites, kinsfolk of the queen from Provence or Savoy, who were richly rewarded with office in England. One of the queen's uncles became lord of the Honour of Richmond in 1240, and another, the hated Boniface, archbishop of Canterbury in 1245. Henry was also noted for his piety, and his attachment to the Papacy came to rouse hostility. Indeed it was the sheer cost of English involvement in papal ventures in Sicily that prompted the great crisis of the reign, the Barons' War of 1258–65.

The barons of England had grown to think of themselves as the natural defenders of the rights of the community. Magna Carta had been re-issued in revised form in 1225, and a plan of constitutional reform that would give some check to the authority of royal officers had been drawn up in 1244. Finally a leader was found for the barons in the person of Simon de Montfort, a "foreign favourite" who had married the king's sister Eleanor in 1238 but who had grown increasingly disaffected during the 1250s. The barons forced the king to agree to a moderate programme of reform embodied in the Provisions of Oxford in 1258, but it proved impossible to set reasonable checks to royal power. Civil war broke out in 1263 and the leadership of Montfort resulted in a resounding baronial victory at Lewes on May 14, 1264. However, it proved equally impossible to run a monarchy

without a king. Both the king and prince Edward, his son and heir, were taken into the equivalent of protective custody, but defections from Montfort's side, coupled with the energy and resource of the young prince Edward (who escaped from custody on May 28, 1265) resulted in Montfort's defeat and death at the battle of Evesham on August 4, 1265.

The last seven years of Henry's reign were spent in reconciliation. Montfort's supporters had been disinherited, an act which prompted savage fighting. By the Dictum of Kenilworth, October 31, 1266, the king asserted his right to exercise his authority without impediment, but made provision, however, for the followers of Earl Simon to redeem their lands. The Statute of Marlborough, issued in the following year, adopted some of

Note: *Shown above is Beaumaris Castle in Anglesey, as it might have appeared if the architect's design had been realised. It was begun in 1295, and left unfinished in the 1320s.*

6. (Facing page) Beaumaris Castle in Anglesey: see the note at the foot of page 12.

Montfort's innovations, and restated the constitutional force of Magna Carta in its 1225 form. Some of the more quarrelsome warriors were diverted to Crusades, and Prince Edward himself crossed the Channel on his way to the Holy Land in August 1270. In the course of the struggle and of the peacemaking that followed a large section of the whole community was drawn into the disputes. Montfort, in January 1265, had held a parliament attended, for the first time, by knights of the shires and burgesses of the towns, summoned in an attempt to gain general support. Thirteenth-century parliaments were occasions when the king took counsel on a wide range of business, judicial, financial and political, and it was a sure sign of the growing importance of the lesser nobility and the townsmen that their presence was needed at these assemblies, even if at this stage their function was no more than to hear and obey what the king and his councillors commanded them.

THE REIGN OF EDWARD I
1272—1307

Edward I was one of the greatest of English kings, strong, intelligent and resourceful. His achievements were permanent and helped to mould the shape of the realm and its institutions for the rest of the Middle Ages.

7. (Right) Twelve crosses were erected by Edward I in memory of his wife Eleanor. Their statuary survives in fair condition at Waltham (Herts) and at Geddington and Hardingstone (Northants).

He was happily married to Eleanor of Castile, and he left an enduring memorial to her after her death at Hadby, Nottinghamshire, in November 1290, in the beautiful series of Eleanor Crosses by which he marked the progress of her body to her tomb at Westminster.

Much of his energy and skill as an organiser and a soldier was spent in an attempt to win control, using the feudal customs of his age where necessary, over the whole of Britain. He was also involved from 1293 onwards in a tangled net of diplomacy and war in France, where he had vital territorial interests in Gascony and the south-west. He achieved outstanding success in Wales. The last of the great princes, Llywelyn ap Gruffudd, was killed in a skirmish in 1282, and the Statute of Wales of 1284 brought the principality of

8. *In parts of England medieval agriculture reached its highest point of prosperity in the course of the thirteenth century. Some great landlords, including ecclesiastical landlords, showed great enterprise in the exploitation of their arable lands.*

Wales under direct royal rule and put an end to any hope of an independent native principality, or even of a native principality linked to the English crown by feudal bonds. Edward's military successes, and the legal and administrative skills of his councillors, would have been useless if not further supplemented by a fearsomely expensive policy of castle-building and by the encouragement of towns in the lee of the fortifications. Great castles such as Beaumaris and Caernarvon and Conway guaranteed permanence—at a cost—to the Edwardian Conquest. Marcher Lords followed (and indeed some had anticipated) a similar policy elsewhere in Wales. Military expertise in the handling of cavalry and archers helped to bring success, and the enlistment of Welsh archers was to prove a con-

Well-run manors with their home farms, open fields, strip cultivation and peasants' plots, produced cereal crops as efficiently as was possible, given the limitations of medieval farming techniques.

15

stant source of strength to English arms in the course of the Hundred Years' War with France, 1337–1453.

Edward was not so successful in Scotland though there were moments even late in his reign when it seemed likely that the Welsh pattern would be repeated. Alexander III of Scotland died in 1286. His heir, recognised as such by the Scottish nobles, was his infant

10. (Right) Stairway branch-
ing off from the east of the north
transept at Wells, leading on right
to the upper Chapter House.

granddaughter, Margaret, the
daughter of the Nor-
wegian king, Eric II. A
marriage alliance was arranged
between the "Maid of Nor-
way" and Edward's son, but
Margaret died on the journey
to Scotland in September
1290. Thereupon the suc-
cession was disputed, and
Edward intervened, claiming
feudal rights as superior lord
of Scotland. He presided
over a judgement in favour of
one of the claimants, John
Balliol, who did homage to
Edward at Newcastle on
December 26, 1292. Balliol
found his position difficult;
the creation of a Scottish–
French alliance prompted full
active English intervention,
and he was defeated and over-
thrown in 1296. Scottish
independent aspirations were

kept alive by William Wallace until his capture and execution in 1305 and then much
more dramatically by Robert Bruce who, though defeated, was still active and dangerous
when Edward died on his last campaign, on July 7, 1307.

Military and political concern with Wales and Scotland and France were important but

9. (Facing page) Salisbury Cathedral was completed except for the West Front and the tower
(added in the following century) between 1220 and 1258. It was built when the town itself was
moved some two miles from its former site at Old Sarum, and is properly regarded as one of the finest
examples of Early English Gothic.

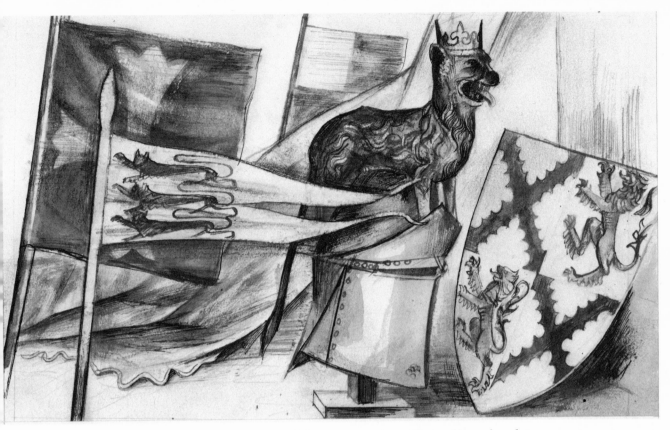

12. (Above) *Heraldry, as a science of armorial bearings, spread rapidly in thirteenth and fourteenth century England, reaching a high point in the reign of Edward III.*

Edward is also remembered rightly as a great law-giver. A number of Statutes, drawn up between 1275 and 1290, reformed the working of law and of administration in matters concerning land (including the lands of the Church), inheritance, feudal service, the rights of freemen to bear arms and what arms they should possess, and the proper practices of trading and merchandise. The statutes were not anti-feudal. The king's interests and the interests of the great barons largely coincided. Edward indeed won general co-operation and approval. An intelligent ruler gave the community the laws it desired. But government undoubtedly became more complicated and also more expensive. Edward had one new advantage. He was the first English king to be able to borrow money on a large scale. The Jews were expelled from England in 1290, but their place as financial experts had already passed to Italians, representing advanced banking companies, especially active in handling English wool exports. Finance also explains why knights and burgesses

11. (Facing page) *On June 24, 1314, at a site some two miles south of Stirling, the main engagement was fought at the Battle of Bannockburn.*
The English forces, led by Edward II himself, were routed by Robert Bruce, and the Scottish pikemen played a prominent part in the victory.

were attending parliaments more frequently; their presence was needed to secure the co-operation of the taxpayer in the shires and the towns. During the last ten years of his reign Edward was rousing more and more hostility because of his financial demands, but his personal prestige was so high that no rebellion was raised against him. He limited discontent by reissuing Magna Carta in its 1225 guise. By the end of his reign the community of England was more sharply defined. Edward was indeed still a feudal monarch, but he was also an effective national king.

14. *(Facing page) Effigies of churchmen and of laymen, barons and knights, were a regular feature of church decoration. Shown here are: background, the effigy of Edward III (died 1377) from Westminster Abbey; centre, a retrospective thirteenth-century effigy of a Saxon bishop in Wells Cathedral; foreground, the effigy of a knight from Dorchester (Oxon) c. 1295—1305.*

ECONOMY AND SOCIETY IN THE THIRTEENTH CENTURY

The economy of England and of most of Western Europe reached a high point in its development in the course of the thirteenth century. The overwhelming majority of people still lived on the land, but this did not mean that society was static and unmoving. There was a substantial increase in population, the population of England at least doubling itself between 1086 and 1300 when it is likely to have reached 3,000,000. London became the outstanding centre with perhaps 30,000 inhabitants and York, Bristol, Plymouth and Coventry were also populous and flourishing. This increase in populations was widespread and had many important social consequences. More land was placed under cultivation. Better techniques of husbandry were introduced, particularly by the larger landowners who benefited most from the expansion. There was much taking-in of land from the extensive

15. *(Facing page) The banqueting hall was the one essential feature of a great house in the later Middle Ages.   This one, built c. 1240, is at Stokesay Castle in Shropshire.*

woodlands and heaths of England.   Marshes were drained, notably in the Fen country and in Romney.   The peasantry benefited in many ways.   The practical distinction between free and unfree became less important: military service and taxation became more an obligation of wealth rather than a matter of simple status.   The landlords benefited even more, and by the end of the century we find many great landlords maintaining and even reviving traditional onerous services (such as plough-service or carting-service) and dues which had in the earlier part of the century been generally commuted for cash.

In general, however, the working of society became increasingly dependent on a money economy.   More currency was in circulation, and attempts were made—not altogether successfully at this stage—to introduce a gold currency by the side of the silver.   International trade increased, above all the trade in wool.   England became a great exporter of wool to the cloth-making centres of Flanders, and it has been estimated that as many as 8,000,000 fleeces were exported annually by 1300.   A native cloth industry also flourished

16. *(Below) Dancing and music-making were important elements in rural and urban life, especially at fairs and great festivals.*

especially in the east and north-east at Northampton, Stamford, Lincoln and Beverley. The scarlet cloth of Lincoln was internationally famous. A whole network of industry sustained these developments, fullers who relied on water-power in new centres in the Lake District and Yorkshire, and dyers as well as weavers. The needs of this growth in the wool trade demanded bigger and better fairs and markets, and the fairs of St. Ives in Huntingdonshire, of Boston and of Stamford became especially well known. Great stimulus was given to urban development, often with the conscious co-operation of the king or the great landlords. The bishop of Winchester alone founded six new towns between 1200 and 1255. The towns, even London, remained much less independent than in parts of Europe, and royal control was generally much in evidence. Privileges

both in matters of government and in trade were granted by charter, and usually fell effectively into the hands of guilds of merchants. The old maxim that "Town air makes a man free" still applied, however, and the thirteenth-century town, though small by modern standards, provided great opportunities for the enterprising.

Increased commercial activity, especially trade overseas, brought with it more sophisticated financial skill. Italian bankers became increasingly influential as they helped support English kings in their wars and in meeting the costs of increased royal government. Internal trade also flourished, and a more buoyant money economy had its effect even in the basic relationship of the king to his tenants-in-chief and of the tenants-in-chief to their feudal tenants. Greater freedom of choice was given to such tenants. They could more easily pay rather than serve in person. More flexible terms of service brought modifications into the feudal order. Money, more advanced forms of government and urban development encouraged the growth of a middle class of officials and lawyers.

Intellectual Life and Architecture

England enjoyed an active intellectual life in the thirteenth century, producing two outstanding scholars in Robert Grosseteste, bishop of Lincoln from 1235 until his death in 1253, and later in the century, Roger Bacon (c. 1220–c. 1292). The universities of Oxford and Cambridge provided educated men for the church and the state, and the typical college system began to appear in Oxford about the middle of the century. Literature of permanent value was produced in the three languages current among scholars, Latin in which were written serious scholarly works in theology and history, Norman French in which courtly romances (often based on English material) were written, and some prose and poetry in Middle English. The outstanding artistic and intellectual achievements were made in the field of architecture. The great churches of Westminster (rebuilt mostly under the patronage of Henry III between 1244 and 1269), Salisbury and much of Lincoln, bear still most eloquent testimony to the power of Gothic ecclesiastical architecture. Towards the end of the century the dominant Early English style gave way to a style generally known as the Decorated, noted for its elegance, richness and greater ornamentation.

17. (Facing page) At Crecy in August 1346 Edward III's army was forced to an open engagement against a French force much superior in numbers. By taking a powerful defensive position, the English king was able to take full advantage of the skill of his archers and dismounted men-at-arms. At close quarters the English long-bow (which had a fire-power almost five times that of the cross-bow) proved devastating, and the French cavalry, trapped in an overwhelming cross-fire, was utterly defeated with heavy losses. The blind king of Bohemia, the Count of Flanders, the Count of Blois and many leading French noblemen died in the battle. 25

THE MONARCHY AND POLITICS IN THE FOURTEENTH CENTURY

Edward I had been one of the strongest and most successful of English kings, but he left a difficult heritage to his successors. Government was expensive, and financial cares were never far from the minds of royal advisers. The kings needed success in war to justify their authority; and success in war again was expensive. There was little questioning of the royal right to rule, but the exaction of money by taxes or other imposts involved a measure of consent on the part of those taxed and of those responsible for its collection.

19. (*Facing page*) *The Black Death is the name given to a new and deadly form of plague, which first reached England, in Dorset, in August 1348, and quickly spread throughout the land. Later attacks in 1361—2 and in 1369 were also notably severe. The fall in population was dramatic though unevenly spread. In some places mortality figures reached as high as a third or a half of the total population, but other areas escaped more lightly.*

26

18. (Facing page) *Bankers flourished in the later Middle Ages, particularly in Italy, where the "Lombards" and the men of Florence became famous for their skill in handling money and the instruments of financial exchange.*

The great men of the realm, the magnates, had a natural right to be consulted. The fourteenth century saw a series of crises in the course of which strong parties among the baronage from time to time claimed an effective role in the processes of royal government, and the shape of medieval Parliament—Lords and Commons—gradually emerged. It was a violent age, more so than the century which preceded it. Politics were played for high stakes, and the losers, king's favourites or barons, were often executed. Two of the four kings of the century were deposed and murdered, Edward II in 1327, and Richard II in 1399–1400. Yet during the middle years of the century England enjoyed a period of political greatness under the warrior king, Edward III (1327–77).

Edward II, already acclaimed as Prince of Wales, succeeded his father Edward I automatically in 1307. He proved himself an incapable ruler. In his early years he relied on

his Gascon favourite, Piers Gaveston, and so roused the fury of a large part of the community against him until the baronage forced the humiliation and execution of Gaveston in 1312. Edward attempted to recover prestige by military operations against Robert Bruce but met with utter disaster at Bannockburn in 1314, a Scottish victory which marked an important stage in the consolidation of the independent Scottish monarchy. The Declaration of Arbroath in 1320 asserted Scottish independence, and in 1323 Edward was forced to agree to a truce with Scotland. After Bannockburn the effective reins of power passed into the hands of the king's cousin, Thomas of Lancaster, the chief of the powerful group of reforming barons, known as the Lords Ordainer. In 1321, however, Edward reasserted himself; Thomas was defeated and executed in 1322; and Edward attempted to rule with the help of the Despenser family. The community turned steadily against him again, including his own wife, Isabella of France, and her lover Roger Mortimer. An effective rising forced Edward to the West Country. He was captured at Neath Abbey in November 1326 and was formally deposed in January 1327, by the nobles, clergy and people, being succeeded by his fourteen-year-old son Edward; Isabella and Mortimer governed in the young king's name. Edward II was murdered that September.

His son's reign, despite its grim beginning, turned to political triumph. Mortimer was executed in 1330, and the queen mother sent to exile in the country. Edward III proved a formidable warrior and leader of soldiers. He inflicted defeats on Scotland, and then in 1337 entered into warfare with France. His own political career at home was clearly tied up with the French war. Brilliant successes in the early stages were followed by later reverses and his long reign closed with troubles and turbulence resulting in the summons of the so-called Good Parliament (in whose long deliberations the Commons played a decisive part) in 1376, a year before Edward's death. The prestige of the monarch stood high. He and his eldest son, the Black Prince, became leaders of the chivalric world. Much intangible strength was added to the monarchy, while the ordinary institutions of royal government, Exchequer, Chancery and the royal Courts of Justice flourished.

There followed an unhappy final reign to close the century when Richard II (1377–99) succeeded his grandfather on the throne, ten years old, and unsuited to the times. He did not lack physical bravery, but was no soldier at a time when military virtues were

needed. He was intelligent, complicated, erratic, again at a time when government called for more straightforward virtues. Constitutional struggles left the barons in command for a while, represented, as they were for the most part, by the Lords Appellant (so called for their success in ordering appeals of treason against some of the powerful friends of the king in 1388). Richard, however, steadily reasserted himself and for the last year of his life attempted to rule as a despot. He went too far when he alienated the most powerful princes of the blood, and forced his own cousin, Henry Bolingbroke of the House of Lancaster, into exile. Henry returned in July 1399 and the whole country, tired of the despot, rallied to him. At first Henry claimed only to be seeking redress of his own grievances but it quickly became apparent that he had to seize the throne: half measures would not do. A meeting of Parliament was called in Richard's name, and the king was formally deposed by the Estates, supported by many Londoners. Richard was imprisoned and died, presumably murdered, at Pontefract in February 1400.

22. (Above) Ornamentation in the great churches was often elaborate. This example from a capital in Southwell Minster depicts a horseman and a goat.

21. (Facing page) Substantial walls and formidable gates were constructed around thriving towns such as London itself, York, Chester and Canterbury.

23. (Below) Misericords, projections on the underside of choir stalls, were arranged so that support could be given even to a standing person. This vivid example is from the Henry VII chapel in Westminster Abbey.

24. (Above) The refectory (124′ × 38′) of the late-12th-century Cistercian abbey at Rievaulx.

THE FIRST STAGES OF THE HUNDRED YEARS' WAR

It was perhaps inevitable that serious warfare should break out between France and England. Both were states at a critical point in development from strong feudal monarchies into national monarchies. Much of the energy of the English kings had been expended on schemes to unite and strengthen the position of England within Britain, and as the English monarchies became stronger, so did the position by which the English king held territories in France as a subordinate of the French king become intolerable. Friction over Edward III's lands in Gascony and the homage he owed to the French crown was an important

Note: *The building of Fountains Abbey, shown in Fig. 25 on the facing page, began in about 1140 and went on for generations; the massive transitional Romanesque of the nave may be contrasted with the Early English beauty of the "Chapel of Nine Altars" (c. 1210—c. 1247), with its slender proportions, lancet windows and pure soaring lines.*

cause of the Hundred Years' War. French support for Scotland, and naval rivalry in the Channel, also contributed to the outbreak. A disputed succession to the French throne provided a supplementary reason for English aggression, and Edward was able to claim not only his rights as a subordinate of the French crown but the very crown itself. Intermittently this became a feature of English royal practice and English kings continued to style themselves Kings of France and of England up to the time of the Napoleonic Wars nearly five hundred years later.

25. (Below) *Fountains Abbey, one of the wealthiest of Cistercian Houses in the Later Middle Ages, prospered greatly as a result of the wool trade. Severe in setting, beautiful in execution, Fountains was also practical in design, with an excellent water supply and drainage system.*

26. (Above) *Medical knowledge was based largely on Greek and Arabic writings transmitted through the great school at Salerno.*

27. (Above) *Textiles were the basis of much prosperity in medieval England. Spinners and weavers are seen at work with the tools of their trade.*

The opening phase of the war resulted in great victories for the English, partly because of their superior leadership and tactics. In the harsh school of the Welsh and Scottish wars they had learned the value of skilled bowmen, fighting in close co-ordination with dismounted knights. The French cavalry proved helpless against them. At Crecy in 1346 the French were routed, and the English went on to capture Calais, a town which remained in their hands to the reign of Mary Tudor in the mid-sixteenth century. Ten years after Crecy the English won an even more spectacular victory at Poitiers when, led by Edward the Black Prince, they captured the French king himself and many of his chief men. The French king John was held in honourable captivity in England for more than seven years and died in captivity in 1364 before the huge ransom demanded was completely paid.

Later in the fourteenth century under Charles V (1364–80) France made good its losses, but the English victories had had a lasting effect on national sentiment and prestige.

28. *(Above) Stone-masons were often crafts-men of high social status, banded together in guilds, and enjoying the use of individual mason's marks.*

Edward III encouraged the romantic and chivalric feelings associated with warfare in the fourteenth century. He arranged tournaments, created the Order of the Garter in 1347, and established his Round Table in 1348 in imitation of the Arthurian romances. The Order of the Garter was to serve as a model for Orders of chivalry throughout the western world. Membership was strictly limited to twenty-six in the original foundation, and elaborate ritual and ceremony quickly became a feature of its organisation.

29 & 30. A carpenter (above right) and a dyer (right), and a weaver (page 34, Fig. 27), were among the craftsmen mentioned by Chaucer in the Canterbury Tales, as members of guilds, each of them "well fit to be an alderman".

31. (Left) By the end of the period a prosperous merchant's house would be well built, well furnished.

ordered medieval structure of rural manor and carefully regulated guild life in towns suffered severely under the strains. Falling prices and rising wages caused a decline in the so-called "high farming" techniques (by which great lords exploited their

ECONOMIC PROBLEMS: FAMINE, PLAGUE AND PEASANT DISCONTENT

There was widespread discontent in fourteenth-century England in comparison with the more stable thirteenth century. Population ceased to rise in the early decades of the century, and fell—in some areas dramatically by as much as fifty per cent—in the second half of the century. There were occasional famines, a severe one as early as 1315–17, and the emergence of a particularly virulent strain of plague, notably the fearsome Black Death of 1348–49, contributed to the decline. The

32. (Right) Communications were never easy, and roads often in disrepair, but one should not exaggerate the isolation of the communities of Western Europe.

demesnes directly) even before the Black Death struck. More land was leased out, and much labour service was commuted for cash payments. Attempts to preserve the old order by government ordinances or by statute were not completely successful. The second half of the fourteenth century saw a greater emancipation of the peasants from labour services, and the emergence of a solid class of yeoman farmers. The Peasants Revolt of 1381 flared up in opposition to the remaining villein services—and also to the new taxation, particularly the Poll Taxes. It did not succeed in its immediate aims but it left a tradition of action to the common people of England.

Discontent was not confined to the countryside and there was much turbulence also in towns where the old guild structures proved inadequate in new social conditions. But all was not stagnation and decay. The wool trade and a native cloth industry flourished. English merchants, especially London merchants, began to play a prominent part in affairs; their fortunes and power rested mostly on wool and textiles.

33. (Above) *Fine gardens were planned and carefully tended in the great baronial houses.*

INTELLECTUAL LIFE IN THE FOURTEENTH CENTURY

England produced many outstanding intellectual figures in the course of the fourteenth century, including William of Ockham, the philosopher, and John Wycliffe, the greatest scholar of the Oxford of his day. Wycliffe's teachings were at times contrary to orthodox belief, but the full force of his work was not felt until after his death in 1384 when many of the unorthodox teachers and preachers, who came to be known as Lollards, looked to his writings for inspiration and found in them justification for their rejection of the church

34. *(Facing page) King's College Chapel, Cambridge, the first stone of which was laid in 1446, was completed in the early sixteenth century. It provides one of the most splendid examples of the Perpendicular style. Founded by Henry VI, who showed great interest in education, it stands as a monument to his generosity.*

system and some of the most important beliefs in which they had been brought up. There was indeed general dissatisfaction with the way the church conducted its business, especially with the friars who had gained a reputation for greed and avarice. The monasteries were not seriously corrupt, but had lost their early reforming zeal. England also became known as a centre for mystics and mystical piety of a religious nature.

During the second half of the century there was a great revival of literary activity in England, a period which saw the triumph of English over French as the language of the

36. (Facing page) Joan of Arc had helped to revitalise the French armies and to persuade the Dauphin to be crowned at Rheims as Charles VII on July 18, 1429. In the following year Joan was captured by the Burgundians, and after trial by the Inquisition handed over to the English to be burned at the stake as a relapsed heretic in 1431.

court and of letters.   Geoffrey Chaucer, a Londoner, urbane, polished and sophisticated, proved to be one of the greatest of all poets in the English language.   His *Canterbury Tales* provides superb insight into the society and people of the age of Richard II.   Fine poetry in alliterative metre was written in the north-west of England, ranging from the long Arthurian romance of *Sir Gawain and the Green Knight* to poems of delicate religious sensitivity such as *Pearl* and *Patience*.   Langland brings us more into touch with the lower orders of society in producing his skilful visionary poem, *Piers the Ploughman*.   Historians and chroniclers still tended to write in Latin, but English prose was growing more flexible: the active support given by Wycliffe and his followers to full translation of the Scriptures and to preaching in English helped to encourage men to write in their native tongue.

Under pressure of nationalist feelings the architects too adopted a bold insular style

in their churches, great and small. The Decorated phase in Gothic architecture gave way to the style we know as Perpendicular, a style that was to dominate English architectural thought in churches for the rest of the Middle Ages through to the early modern period. Its characteristics are a blend of straight, often soaring, lines with ogee curves. The rebuilding of the Choir at Gloucester Cathedral after the burial there of Edward II is sometimes seen as the creative origin of the style which remained essentially English. Other fine examples are to be found in the Choir and the Presbytery at York, and at Canterbury.

THE HOUSE OF LANCASTER: THE LAST STAGES OF THE HUNDRED YEARS' WAR

Henry Bolingbroke in the early stages of his revolt against Richard II in 1399 claimed to be fighting for his right to succeed to the inheritance left by his father, John of Gaunt, Duke of Lancaster, third son of Edward III. His successes quickly led him beyond that. Richard II surrendered to him, and on September 29 resigned his throne. Henry succeeded with the support of the great barons and of the Commons in Parliament. His reign was on the whole very successful. He faced and ultimately overcame the most serious Welsh revolt of the Late Middle Ages, led by Owain Glyndwr, and also suppressed a serious Northern rebellion led by the Percy family and by Archbishop Scrope of York. His career was clouded, however, by personal illness after 1406, and by financial worries. Although he had been one of the wealthiest of the great lords of England his financial fortunes were diminished rather than increased after his accession to the throne. The Commons were reluctant to grant the taxation that the Crown really needed. His problems were made less difficult by the weakness of France (where the king, Charles VI, was subject to occasional bouts of insanity) and Scotland (whose king, James I, was a captive in English hands from 1406 to 1424). In the later stages of his reign his eldest son, the young prince Henry—in spite of a reputation for wild living—played an increasingly active part in affairs.

In 1413 Prince Henry, then aged twenty-six, succeeded his father on the throne as Henry V. He has left a tremendous name behind him as the very type of patriot warrior-king. He renewed claims to the French throne, invaded Normandy with a small but highly efficient army of men-at-arms and archers, and at Agincourt utterly routed the flower of French chivalry at odds of some eight to one. He married Catherine, the

37. *(Facing page) Minster Lovell, a handsome manor house, was rebuilt by the Lovell family in the fifteenth century on the banks of the river Windrush in Oxfordshire.*

daughter of Charles VI of France, and by the Treaty of Troyes in 1420 was recognised as Heir to and Regent of France. His new interest in French affairs seemed overwhelmingly successful. Normandy was held firmly by the English army. It seemed likely that a joint kingdom dominated by English interest was going to emerge from the Hundred Years' War. At the early age of thirty-five, however, Henry V died and the next generation saw the undoing of his political work.

Even now it is not easy to judge this heroic figure of Henry V. Some blame him for reopening the French war but against that he undoubtedly strengthened English feeling and unity as few rulers have ever done. In domestic affairs—partly because of his success in arms—he achieved much. His Council was loyal and his Parliament obedient. He did much to ensure the stabilisation of the Lancastrian dynasty, though he left a perilous

heritage to his infant son, Henry, recognised by the terms of the Treaty of Troyes as king of France as well as king of England.

Responsibility for looking after the interests of the new dynasty rested especially on the shoulders of Henry V's two brothers, John, Duke of Bedford (who died in 1435) and Humphrey, Duke of Gloucester. In spite of their ability they were on the whole unsuccessful. Victories in France had depended on the disunity that racked the French kingdom, particularly the violent feud between the Capetian dynasty and the Burgundians. Very slowly the French factions were brought together. Joan of Arc rallied the royalists, and succeeded in getting the cowardly, dilatory Dauphin crowned at Rheims in 1429. The following year she was betrayed to the Burgundians and burned as a heretic by the English at Rouen. At long last in 1435 the Burgundians made peace with the French royalists and from that point on the English cause was doomed. Men were thinking now in terms of "England" and "France", and grandiose ideas of a joint Anglo-French kingdom fell on

stony ground.   The French began to learn from their earlier defeats, built up an efficient and well-financed army, even developing an effective artillery arm.   Bravery and tenacity kept the English cause alive for a while but in 1453 they suffered final defeat.   Only Calais was left in their possession out of all their vast agglomeration of territories in France.

England suffered much in her internal affairs during these last phases of the Hundred Years' War.   The minority of Henry VI was followed by a period of weak rule in the course of which power passed into the hands of court factions.   Even so, one must not exaggerate. There was still much respect for royal authority and much healthy development in organisation of the royal council and of parliament.   But Henry VI himself was a gentle, incompetent man quite incapable of exercising royal authority in that turbulent age, a complete contrast to his father.   His uncles and other councillors did their best, but the court tended to split into factions, particularly after the death (probably the murder) of the king's last surviving uncle, Humphrey, Duke of Gloucester, in 1447.

THE WARS OF THE ROSES: LANCASTER AND YORK

The loss of French possessions increased the rivalries and hatreds among the English nobility.   The royal house was divided against itself.   In October 1453 Henry VI's queen gave birth to a son, Edward, an heir to the Lancastrian throne, but King Henry was already suffering from his first severe attack of insanity which was to incapacitate him completely until the end of 1454.   In the meantime Richard, Duke of York, the nearest male heir after the infant Prince Edward, was appointed Protector.   Henry VI recovered; but Richard and his friends, the Yorkists, could not bear to give up their power and wealth, and civil war broke out in 1455.   There is no contemporary justification for the name "Wars of the Roses" given to the faction fights and palace intrigues of the succeeding thirty years; but the term is useful and gives the essential feeling of division between two branches of the royal dynasty, the House of Lancaster with its Red Rose symbol, and the White Rose of the House of York.   Richard of York was killed in battle at Wakefield in 1460 just when a Yorkist victory seemed in sight, but his son Edward was acclaimed king as Edward IV in the following year, defeated the royal forces and eventually imprisoned the pathetic Henry VI in the Tower in 1465.   In 1470–71 there was a brief, even more pathetic, Lancastrian restoration, largely because the powerful Richard Neville, Earl of Warwick, deserted the

38.   (Facing page)   William Caxton printed his first books in Bruges, but later set up his printing shop at Westminster in 1476 and produced the first printed books in England including Chaucer's Canterbury Tales, Gower's Confessio Amantis *and Malory's* Morte d'Arthur.   *Some were superbly illustrated with woodcuts.*

Yorkist cause for the Lancastrian, but Edward IV, after a spell in exile, won a decisive victory at Tewkesbury on May 4, 1471. The Lancastrian heir, Prince Edward, was killed, the queen, the formidable Margaret of Anjou, was imprisoned, and the poor Henry VI himself died (possibly by violence) in the Tower. Flickers of rebellion continued (causing, for example, the execution of Edward IV's brother, the Duke of Clarence, in 1478) but Edward IV ruled powerfully and effectively until his death at the age of sixty in 1483. He did much to restore the prestige of the monarchy and to establish the foundation of strong conciliar government which was to be the hallmark of the New Monarchy of the sixteenth century. He was succeeded briefly by his young son Edward V, but the throne was quickly usurped by the prince's uncle, Richard, Duke of Gloucester, who became Richard III. At some stage (the actual date and the manner of their deaths are unknown), the young Edward V and his brother died in the Tower.

Richard III was a powerful ruler, a good soldier and administrator, but he never gained the full loyalty of the people, and in 1485 England was invaded by the Lancastrain heir, Henry Tudor. Richard was killed, fighting bravely to the end, at the battle of Bosworth on Monday, August 22. Henry's victory and subsequent marriage to the Yorkist heiress, Elizabeth, brought to an end this turbulent period of dynastic uncertainty and faction fight.

ECONOMIC REVIVAL AND INTELLECTUAL LIFE IN FIFTEENTH-CENTURY ENGLAND

The population of England seems slowly to have risen from its low point at the end of the fourteenth century, though in 1485 it was still below the probable figure for 1300. Agriculture showed little signs of prosperity until late in the century, though there was an increase in the freeing of the villeins which held much hope for the future. It would be wrong to think, however, that the fifteenth century was a time of continuous decline. The wool trade and the cloth trade flourished. Merchants gained privileges and commercial advantages in the Baltic and, to some extent, in the Mediterranean. The best evidence of the prosperity of the sheep areas, notably East Anglia and the Cotswolds, comes from the magnificent parish churches that were built or added to during this century.

There was an undoubted decline in intellectual production after the so-called "Age of Chaucer". Sir Thomas Malory's *Morte d'Arthur* (a vigorous collection in English of the

39. (*Facing page*) *Economic revival brought increased prosperity especially to merchants involved in overseas trade. Great wool merchants and clothiers also thrived. Families such as the Paycockes of Coggeshall, the Grevels of Chipping Camden, the Laurences of Ludlow and Stokesay and the Pulteneys of London and Penshurst left memorials in their domestic buildings to the new wealth of the age.*

Arthurian legends) and some of the miracle and morality plays written for and performed by guilds in the towns show outstanding quality, but poetry and prose generally, in Latin and in English, rarely rises above the mediocre.

In architecture the Perpendicular still preserved its popularity and some features, such as fan-vaulting (already well developed in the preceding century), reached their finest form. Domestic architecture also mellowed. In spite of the turbulence among the upper nobility society itself was growing more peaceful. Technical reasons contributed to making the powerful castle, built primarily for defence, old fashioned: the development of artillery made the old style of siege warfare antiquated. As towns developed, some merchant wealth went into the building of fine town houses.

The Universities of Oxford and Cambridge grew in stature and prestige. Great care was spent on the building of new colleges. Henry VI was an active patron.

The general standard of literacy improved, and technical advances, started on the Continent, began to affect English life. In 1476 William Caxton, with a prosperous career in commerce behind him, set up his printing press in London. England, and especially its capital city of London, was beginning to enjoy the full effects of the Renaissance in learning and letters, so much a feature of life in Italy and the Low Countries in the second half of the fifteenth century.